2024

EMERGING TECHNOLOGIES

THAT WILL CHANGE THE WORLD

NAVIGATING THE FUTURE OF INNOVATION AND WHAT LIES BEYOND

HARPER PIPER

Copyright HARPER PIPER, 2024.

All rights reserved. No part of this publication may be reproduced, distributed, or transmitted in any form or by any means, including photocopying, recording, or other electronic or mechanical methods, without the prior written permission of the publisher, except in the case of brief quotations embodied in critical reviews and certain other non-commercial uses permitted by copyright law.

Table of Contents

Introduction to Emerging Technologies _____ 9

Chapter 1 _____ 15

    Artificial General Intelligence (AGI) _____ 15

Chapter 2 _____ 23

    CRISPR Gene Editing _____ 23

Chapter 3 _____ 31

    Quantum Computing _____ 31

Chapter 4 _____ 41

    Brain-Computer Interfaces _____ 41

Chapter 5 _____ 49

    Humanoid Robots _____ 49

Chapter 6 _____ 57

    Generative AI _____ 57

Chapter 7 _____ 65

    Starlink Satellites and Internet _____ 65

Chapter 8 _____ 73

    Artificial Wombs _____ 73

Chapter 9	*81*
Nanotechnology	81
Chapter 10	*91*
Internet of Things (IoT)	91
Chapter 11	*101*
Autonomous Vehicles	101
Chapter 12	*111*
Space Tourism	111
Chapter 13	*119*
Smart Cities	119
Chapter 14	*127*
Mixed Reality	127
Chapter 15	*135*
3D Printing	135
Chapter 16	*143*
Fusion Power	143
Chapter 17	*151*
Blockchain Technology	151
Chapter 18	*159*
Solid-State Batteries	159
Conclusion	*167*

Introduction to Emerging Technologies

In the ever-evolving landscape of technological advancement, the dawn of the 21st century has witnessed a remarkable surge in innovations that are reshaping the way we perceive and interact with the world around us. From Artificial General Intelligence (AGI) to Quantum Computing, from CRISPR Gene Editing to Brain-Computer Interfaces, a plethora of emerging technologies are not only transforming industries but also challenging the very fabric of human existence. This introduction sets the stage for exploring these groundbreaking advancements and their profound implications on society.

At the forefront of this technological revolution is Artificial General Intelligence (AGI), a concept that envisions machines with the cognitive abilities to understand, learn, and adapt autonomously, akin to human beings. Unlike narrow AI, which is designed for specific tasks, AGI possesses the potential to tackle a diverse range of cognitive challenges, from scientific research to creative endeavors. Spearheaded by leading organizations such as OpenAI and Google DeepMind, research in AGI is making significant strides, fueled by advancements in deep learning, neural networks, and reinforcement learning. The pursuit of AGI raises profound questions about the nature of intelligence, consciousness, and the ethical implications of creating machines that rival or surpass human capabilities.

Complementing the advancements in AI is CRISPR Gene Editing, a revolutionary technique that allows scientists to precisely alter the genetic code of organisms. CRISPR-Cas9, often likened to molecular scissors, offers unprecedented capabilities for correcting genetic defects, modifying traits, and even reshaping the evolutionary trajectory of species. While heralded as a potential panacea for genetic disorders and a catalyst for personalized medicine, CRISPR also raises ethical dilemmas surrounding genetic enhancement, designer babies, and the unintended consequences of manipulating the very essence of life.

In the realm of computing, Quantum Computing stands as a beacon of hope for unlocking unprecedented computational power. Harnessing the principles of quantum mechanics, quantum computers promise to solve complex problems at speeds inconceivable to classical computers. From cryptography to drug discovery, quantum computing holds the key to revolutionizing various fields, albeit accompanied by formidable technical challenges and uncertainties. The race towards building practical quantum computers underscores the transformative potential of this emerging technology and its implications for cybersecurity, scientific research, and beyond.

Meanwhile, the convergence of neuroscience and technology has given rise to Brain-Computer Interfaces (BCIs), blurring the boundaries between mind and machine. By decoding neural signals and translating them into actionable commands, BCIs offer new avenues for restoring mobility to the paralyzed, augmenting human capabilities, and even interfacing with artificial intelligence. While still in its infancy, the rapid progress in BCIs heralds a future where the boundaries between human and machine dissolve, raising profound questions about identity, privacy, and the very nature of consciousness.

In the realm of robotics, Humanoid Robots are making strides towards emulating human-like dexterity and cognition. From Boston Dynamics' agile robots to Tesla's autonomous vehicles, these mechanical marvels are reshaping industries, from manufacturing to healthcare. With advancements in machine learning, sensor technology, and material science, humanoid robots are poised to become indispensable collaborators in various domains, from space exploration to elder care.

Generative AI, another frontier in artificial intelligence, is pushing the boundaries of creativity and expression. By training on vast datasets, generative AI systems can create realistic images, videos, and even music, blurring the line between human and machine-generated content. As generative AI continues to evolve, its impact on creative industries, media consumption, and cultural production is poised to be profound, challenging notions of authorship, authenticity, and artistic expression.

These are just a few glimpses into the kaleidoscope of emerging technologies that are reshaping our world at an unprecedented pace. From space tourism to smart cities, from 3D printing to solid-state batteries, the possibilities are as limitless as they are awe-inspiring. As we embark on this journey of exploration and innovation, it is essential to navigate the ethical, societal, and existential implications of these technologies with wisdom, foresight, and empathy. For in the crucible of technological advancement lies the potential to redefine what it means to be human and chart a course towards a more equitable, sustainable, and enlightened future.

Chapter 1

Artificial General Intelligence (AGI)

1. Definition and Concept

Artificial General Intelligence (AGI) represents the pinnacle of artificial intelligence research, aiming to create machines that possess human-like cognitive abilities across a wide range of tasks. Unlike narrow AI systems, which excel at specific tasks within predefined boundaries, AGI aims to replicate the general problem-solving capabilities and adaptability of the human mind.

At its core, AGI seeks to imbue machines with the capacity to understand complex information, learn from experience, reason, plan, and ultimately exhibit flexible intelligence comparable to, or even surpassing, human intelligence. This broad spectrum of capabilities enables AGI systems to autonomously tackle novel challenges, adapt to unforeseen circumstances, and generalize knowledge across diverse domains, much like proficient human beings.

The concept of AGI raises profound philosophical questions about the nature of intelligence, consciousness, and the potential boundaries of artificial systems. It challenges traditional notions of what it means to be intelligent and whether machines can truly exhibit creativity, intuition, and self-awareness akin to sentient beings.

2. Current Research and Developments

The pursuit of AGI has captivated the imaginations of researchers, scientists, and technologists for decades, driving relentless innovation and exploration in the field of artificial intelligence. While achieving true AGI remains an elusive goal, significant strides have been made in various areas of research, laying the groundwork for future breakthroughs.

Deep Learning and Neural Networks: One of the most promising avenues towards AGI lies in deep learning and neural networks, which mimic the structure and function of the human brain. Through the use of artificial neural networks with multiple layers of interconnected nodes, researchers have achieved remarkable progress in tasks such as image recognition, natural language processing, and game playing. Continual advancements in model architectures, training techniques, and computational resources have propelled the capabilities of deep learning systems towards more complex cognitive tasks.

Reinforcement Learning: Another promising approach to AGI is reinforcement learning, inspired by the principles of operant conditioning in psychology. In reinforcement learning, agents learn to maximize cumulative rewards by interacting with their environment and receiving feedback on their actions. Through trial and error, reinforcement learning algorithms can acquire sophisticated decision-making abilities and adapt to dynamic environments. Recent breakthroughs in reinforcement learning, such as AlphaGo's victory over human Go champions and OpenAI's achievements in complex game environments, showcase the potential of this approach for achieving AGI.

Hybrid Approaches: Many researchers advocate for hybrid approaches that combine multiple AI techniques, such as symbolic reasoning, probabilistic inference, and neural computation, to overcome the limitations of individual methods. By leveraging the complementary strengths of different paradigms, hybrid AGI systems aim to achieve a more comprehensive understanding of the world and exhibit more robust intelligence.

Interdisciplinary Research: The quest for AGI transcends traditional boundaries of computer science and encompasses interdisciplinary collaboration with fields such as cognitive science, neuroscience, philosophy, and psychology. By drawing insights from the study of human cognition and consciousness, researchers hope to gain deeper insights into the underlying principles of intelligence and develop more human-like AI systems.

OpenAI, Google DeepMind, and other leading research organizations have spearheaded efforts to advance the frontier of AGI research, investing substantial resources in ambitious projects aimed at pushing the boundaries of artificial intelligence. Despite the significant progress made thus far, achieving AGI remains an immensely challenging task fraught with technical, ethical, and societal complexities.

3. Potential Implications and Applications

The realization of AGI holds transformative implications across a myriad of domains, from healthcare and education to finance and entertainment. The versatility and adaptability of AGI systems open up new frontiers of innovation and possibilities, revolutionizing how we work, live, and interact with technology.

Medical Diagnosis and Treatment: AGI-powered diagnostic systems could revolutionize healthcare by offering accurate and timely assessments of medical conditions, enabling early detection of diseases and personalized treatment plans. By analyzing vast amounts of patient data and medical literature, AGI systems could assist healthcare professionals in making informed decisions and improving patient outcomes.

Scientific Research and Discovery: AGI has the potential to accelerate scientific progress by automating tedious tasks, uncovering hidden patterns in data, and generating novel hypotheses for exploration. From drug discovery and materials science to astrophysics and genomics, AGI systems could aid researchers in solving complex problems and unlocking new insights into the mysteries of the universe.

Autonomous Vehicles and Transportation: AGI-powered autonomous vehicles could revolutionize transportation systems by offering safer, more efficient, and more convenient mobility solutions. By integrating advanced perception, planning, and decision-making capabilities, AGI systems could navigate complex environments, anticipate hazards, and adapt to changing conditions, paving the way for a future of driverless cars, drones, and smart transportation networks.

Personalized Education and Learning: AGI-based tutoring systems could provide personalized learning experiences tailored to individual students' needs, preferences, and learning styles. By adapting instructional content and pacing in real-time, AGI tutors could optimize learning outcomes, address misconceptions, and foster critical thinking skills, democratizing access to high-quality education.

Creative Arts and Entertainment: AGI systems could push the boundaries of creativity in the realms of art, music, literature, and gaming. By generating original compositions, artworks, stories, and virtual worlds, AGI-powered creative tools could inspire new forms of expression, collaboration, and entertainment, blurring the lines between human and machine-generated content.

Ethical and Societal Considerations: The advent of AGI raises profound ethical questions about the implications of delegating decision-making authority to autonomous systems and the potential impact on human society. Concerns about job displacement, economic inequality, algorithmic bias, and existential risks pose formidable challenges that require careful consideration and proactive mitigation strategies.

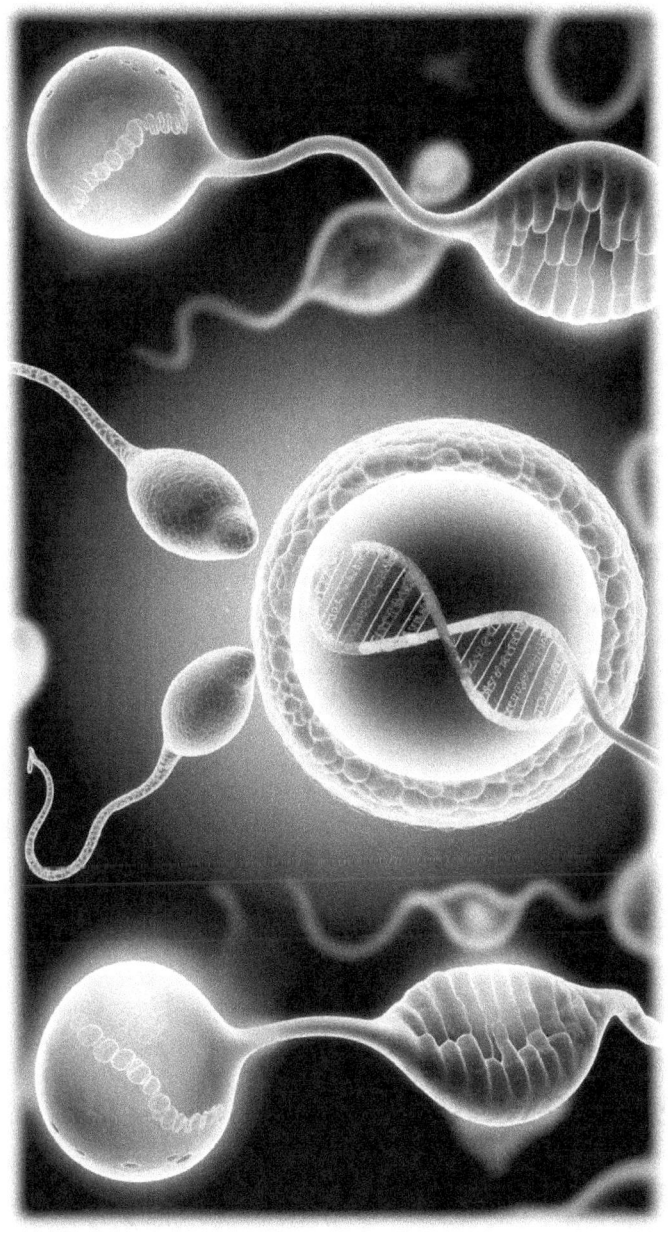

Chapter 2

CRISPR Gene Editing

1. Overview of Gene Editing

Gene editing represents a revolutionary tool in biotechnology, enabling precise modifications to the genetic code of organisms. At its core, gene editing involves altering the DNA sequence of a cell or organism to achieve desired changes, such as correcting genetic defects, introducing beneficial traits, or studying gene function.

Traditional methods of gene editing, such as zinc finger nucleases (ZFNs) and transcription activator-like effector nucleases (TALENs), have paved the way for targeted genetic modifications. However, these techniques are often complex, labor-intensive, and expensive, limiting their widespread adoption.

The advent of Clustered Regularly Interspaced Short Palindromic Repeats (CRISPR) technology has revolutionized the field of gene editing, offering a simpler, more efficient, and versatile approach. CRISPR systems, derived from the bacterial immune response to viral infections, utilize RNA-guided nucleases to precisely target specific DNA sequences for cleavage and modification.

2. CRISPR-Cas9 Technology

CRISPR-Cas9, the most widely used and studied CRISPR system, consists of two main components: the Cas9 enzyme and a guide RNA (gRNA). The gRNA serves as a molecular "address" that directs the Cas9 enzyme to the target DNA sequence, where it induces a double-stranded break (DSB).

Once the DSB is created, the cell's natural repair mechanisms come into play, leading to one of two outcomes: non-homologous end joining (NHEJ) or homology-directed repair (HDR). NHEJ often results in random insertions or deletions at the site of the break, leading to gene disruption or loss of function. HDR, on the other hand, can be harnessed to introduce specific genetic changes by providing a DNA template with the desired sequence.

The simplicity and efficiency of the CRISPR-Cas9 system have democratized gene editing, empowering researchers worldwide to explore a wide range of applications across various organisms, including bacteria, plants, animals, and even humans. From basic research and biotechnology to medicine and agriculture, CRISPR-Cas9 holds immense potential for transforming diverse fields.

3. Medical Applications

CRISPR-Cas9 has sparked tremendous excitement in the medical community due to its potential for treating genetic disorders, preventing hereditary diseases, and revolutionizing personalized medicine.

One of the most promising applications of CRISPR-Cas9 is in the treatment of monogenic disorders, which are caused by mutations in a single gene. Diseases such as sickle cell anemia, cystic fibrosis, and muscular dystrophy present prime targets for CRISPR-mediated gene editing, as correcting the underlying genetic defect could potentially alleviate symptoms or cure the condition altogether.

In addition to monogenic disorders, CRISPR-Cas9 holds promise for treating complex diseases with a genetic component, such as cancer. By targeting oncogenes or tumor suppressor genes implicated in cancer development, CRISPR-based therapies could disrupt tumor growth, enhance the efficacy of existing treatments, and overcome drug resistance.

Furthermore, CRISPR-Cas9 offers opportunities for engineering immune cells, such as T cells, to enhance their ability to recognize and destroy cancer cells. By modifying key genes involved in immune response pathways, researchers can bolster the immune system's ability to mount a robust anti-tumor response, leading to more effective immunotherapies.

Beyond disease treatment, CRISPR-Cas9 has potential applications in disease prevention, genetic screening, and reproductive medicine. Prenatal diagnosis of genetic disorders, correction of disease-causing mutations in embryos, and prevention of hereditary diseases through germline editing are all areas of active research and debate.

4. Ethical Considerations

While CRISPR-Cas9 holds tremendous promise for advancing human health and alleviating suffering, it also raises complex ethical, social, and regulatory questions that must be addressed with care and deliberation.

One of the most pressing ethical concerns surrounding CRISPR-Cas9 is the potential for off-target effects, unintended mutations, and unforeseen consequences. Despite advances in CRISPR technology and bioinformatics tools for predicting off-target activity, the risk of unintended alterations to the genome remains a significant challenge that must be mitigated through rigorous safety testing and validation.

Another ethical dilemma arises from the prospect of germline editing, which involves making heritable changes to the human genome that are passed on to future generations. While germline editing holds the potential to eradicate genetic diseases and enhance human health, it also raises concerns about the potential for unintended consequences, the creation of designer babies, and the exacerbation of social inequalities.

Furthermore, the equitable access to CRISPR-based therapies, the affordability of treatment, and the distribution of benefits and risks are paramount considerations that must be addressed to ensure that gene editing technologies serve the interests of all individuals and communities, regardless of socioeconomic status or geographical location.

In addition to medical applications, CRISPR-Cas9 has implications for agriculture, environmental conservation, and biosecurity, raising questions about the ethical use of gene editing in non-human organisms and ecosystems.

Chapter 3

Quantum Computing

Introduction to Quantum Computing

Quantum computing stands at the forefront of technological innovation, promising to revolutionize computation by harnessing the principles of quantum mechanics. Unlike classical computers, which rely on bits to represent information as either 0 or 1, quantum computers leverage quantum bits, or qubits, which can exist in multiple states simultaneously due to the phenomenon of superposition. This fundamental difference enables quantum computers to perform certain calculations exponentially faster than their classical counterparts, unlocking unprecedented computational power and capabilities.

At the heart of quantum computing is the concept of quantum entanglement, whereby the states of two or more qubits become correlated in such a way that the state of one qubit instantaneously influences the state of the others, regardless of the distance between them. This phenomenon allows quantum computers to perform parallel computations and solve complex problems with remarkable efficiency.

Despite their immense potential, quantum computers remain in the nascent stages of development, with many technical and practical challenges yet to be overcome. Building and operating quantum computers requires overcoming formidable obstacles such as decoherence, which occurs when qubits lose their quantum properties due to interactions with the environment, leading to errors in calculations. Moreover, quantum computers require highly specialized hardware, ultra-low temperatures, and sophisticated control systems to maintain the delicate quantum states of their qubits.

Potential Impact on Cryptography

One of the most widely anticipated applications of quantum computing is its potential to revolutionize cryptography, the science of secure communication. Many of the cryptographic protocols used today, such as RSA and ECC, rely on the difficulty of certain mathematical problems, such as integer factorization and discrete logarithms, to ensure the security of encrypted data.

However, quantum computers have the ability to solve these problems exponentially faster than classical computers using algorithms such as Shor's algorithm. As a result, the cryptographic schemes that underpin the security of the internet, e-commerce, and digital communication are vulnerable to attack by quantum computers, posing a significant threat to cybersecurity and data privacy.

In anticipation of this looming threat, researchers are actively exploring post-quantum cryptography, which involves developing cryptographic algorithms that are resistant to attacks by quantum computers. These algorithms leverage mathematical problems that are believed to be hard even for quantum computers to solve, such as lattice-based cryptography, code-based cryptography, and multivariate polynomial cryptography.

Transitioning to post-quantum cryptographic standards is a complex and multifaceted process that involves extensive research, standardization efforts, and collaboration across academia, industry, and government. While progress has been made in identifying promising candidate algorithms and protocols, widespread adoption of post-quantum cryptography requires careful consideration of factors such as interoperability, usability, and scalability.

Potential Impact on Drug Discovery

Beyond cryptography, quantum computing has the potential to revolutionize the field of drug discovery and development, offering new tools and techniques for accelerating the search for novel therapeutics and treatments. The process of drug discovery involves identifying and optimizing small molecules or biologics that can modulate biological targets associated with diseases.

Quantum computers can simulate the behavior of molecules and proteins at the quantum level, providing insights into their structure, dynamics, and interactions that are inaccessible to classical computers. By leveraging quantum algorithms such as variational quantum eigensolver (VQE) and quantum approximate optimization algorithm (QAOA), researchers can explore the vast space of chemical compounds and predict their properties with unprecedented accuracy.

Quantum computers hold the potential to revolutionize virtual screening, molecular docking, and quantum chemistry calculations, enabling researchers to identify promising drug candidates more efficiently and cost-effectively. Moreover, quantum computing can facilitate the design of custom molecules with desired properties, optimize drug formulations for enhanced efficacy and safety, and accelerate the process of clinical trials and regulatory approval.

Despite the promise of quantum computing in drug discovery, significant challenges remain to be addressed, including the development of scalable quantum algorithms, the integration of quantum and classical computational workflows, and the validation of quantum-derived predictions through experimental validation. Additionally, the practical implementation of quantum computing in pharmaceutical research requires overcoming technical barriers such as qubit error rates, coherence times, and noise mitigation strategies.

Future Developments and Challenges

Looking ahead, the future of quantum computing holds immense promise and potential for transformative impact across a wide range of fields, from cryptography and drug discovery to optimization, machine learning, and beyond. As researchers continue to make advances in hardware, software, and algorithms, the capabilities of quantum computers are expected to grow exponentially, unlocking new frontiers of exploration and innovation.

In the realm of hardware, efforts are underway to develop fault-tolerant quantum computers capable of performing error-corrected computations over extended periods of time. Breakthroughs in qubit coherence, error correction, and fault tolerance are essential for scaling up quantum computing systems and realizing their full potential for practical applications.

On the software and algorithmic front, researchers are exploring new quantum algorithms, protocols, and methodologies for solving a diverse range of problems more efficiently and accurately than classical methods. Quantum machine learning, quantum optimization, and quantum simulation are areas of active research that hold promise for addressing real-world challenges in areas such as logistics, finance, and materials science.

Despite the rapid progress and excitement surrounding quantum computing, significant technical, practical, and theoretical challenges remain to be overcome. Decoherence, qubit connectivity, gate fidelity, and noise remain major obstacles that hinder the scalability and reliability of quantum computers. Moreover, the development of quantum software, programming languages, and debugging tools lags behind hardware advancements, limiting the accessibility and usability of quantum computing technology.

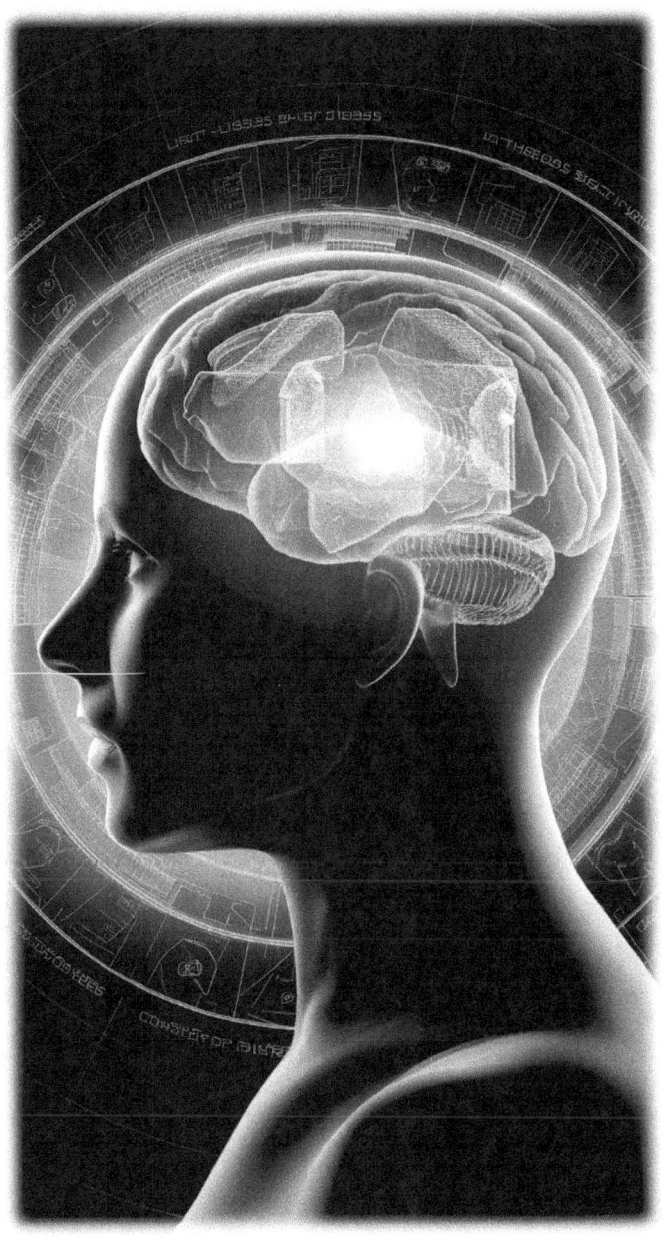

Chapter 4

Brain-Computer Interfaces

How Neuralink and Similar Technologies Work

Brain-computer interfaces (BCIs) represent a groundbreaking fusion of neuroscience, engineering, and computer science, enabling direct communication between the human brain and external devices. These interfaces bridge the gap between the brain's neural signals and digital information, opening up new possibilities for controlling computers, prosthetic limbs, and other devices through pure thought.

Neuralink, founded by entrepreneur Elon Musk, has emerged as a prominent player in the field of brain-computer interfaces, aiming to develop high-bandwidth, minimally invasive neural interfaces that can be implanted in the brain. The core technology behind Neuralink's interfaces involves a network of ultrafine electrodes, or "threads," that are implanted into the brain's cortex to record and stimulate neural activity.

The threads are thinner than a human hair and are designed to interface with large populations of neurons, enabling bidirectional communication with the brain. By detecting and decoding neural signals associated with specific thoughts, movements, or sensations, Neuralink's interfaces can translate these signals into digital commands that can be used to control external devices or software applications.

The implantation process involves inserting the threads into the brain using a minimally invasive surgical procedure, guided by advanced robotics and neuroimaging techniques to ensure precision and safety. Once implanted, the electrodes form stable connections with neural tissue, allowing for long-term recording and stimulation of brain activity.

In addition to recording neural signals, Neuralink's interfaces are capable of delivering precise electrical stimulation to targeted regions of the brain, enabling therapeutic interventions for neurological disorders such as Parkinson's disease, epilepsy, and depression. By modulating neural activity, these interventions can alleviate symptoms, restore function, and improve quality of life for patients.

Beyond Neuralink, other research institutions and companies are also developing innovative brain-computer interface technologies using a variety of approaches. These include non-invasive techniques such as electroencephalography (EEG), magnetoencephalography (MEG), and functional near-infrared spectroscopy (fNIRS), which measure brain activity from outside the skull using electrodes or sensors placed on the scalp or scalp.

While non-invasive BCIs offer advantages in terms of safety, ease of use, and accessibility, they typically have lower spatial resolution and signal quality compared to invasive techniques like Neuralink's implants. As a result, non-invasive BCIs are often used for applications such as brain-computer communication, neurofeedback training, and assistive technology for individuals with disabilities.

Medical Applications

Brain-computer interfaces hold immense promise for a wide range of medical applications, from restoring lost function to the treatment of neurological and psychiatric disorders.

One of the most compelling applications of BCIs is in the field of neuroprosthetics, where brain-controlled devices are used to restore movement, sensation, and communication in individuals with paralysis or limb loss. By decoding neural signals associated with movement intentions, BCIs can enable users to control prosthetic limbs, exoskeletons, or computer cursors with remarkable precision and dexterity, restoring independence and mobility.

BCIs also hold potential for treating neurological disorders such as Parkinson's disease, epilepsy, and chronic pain. By delivering targeted electrical stimulation to specific brain regions, BCIs can modulate neural activity and disrupt abnormal patterns associated with disease symptoms. For example, deep brain stimulation (DBS) implants have been used to alleviate tremors, rigidity, and dyskinesias in patients with Parkinson's disease, offering significant improvements in quality of life.

Furthermore, BCIs have shown promise for cognitive rehabilitation and neurofeedback training in individuals recovering from stroke, traumatic brain injury, or neurodegenerative diseases. By providing real-time feedback on brain activity, BCIs can help patients learn to modulate their brain states and improve cognitive function, memory, and attention.

In the field of mental health, BCIs hold potential for diagnosing and treating psychiatric disorders such as depression, anxiety, and post-traumatic stress disorder (PTSD). By monitoring neural biomarkers associated with mood and emotion, BCIs can provide objective measures of mental health status and guide personalized interventions such as neurofeedback, transcranial magnetic stimulation (TMS), or closed-loop brain stimulation.

Future Possibilities

Looking ahead, the future of brain-computer interfaces holds immense promise for unlocking new frontiers of human potential, understanding, and interaction.

One exciting possibility is the development of **"mind-reading"** technologies that can decode complex thoughts, memories, and emotions directly from neural activity. By analyzing patterns of brain activity associated with specific mental states, BCIs could enable individuals to communicate silently, share experiences, or even transfer knowledge directly from one brain to another.

Moreover, BCIs hold potential for enhancing human cognition and performance through techniques such as neuroenhancement, neurofeedback training, and cognitive augmentation. By modulating brain activity patterns associated with attention, memory, and decision-making, BCIs could enhance learning, creativity, and problem-solving abilities, unlocking new levels of human intelligence and creativity.

BCIs also hold promise for enabling new forms of human-computer interaction, immersive virtual reality experiences, and augmented reality applications. By integrating brain signals with digital interfaces, BCIs could enable users to control virtual avatars, manipulate virtual objects, and interact with digital environments using nothing but their thoughts, blurring the boundaries between the physical and digital worlds.

However, realizing the full potential of brain-computer interfaces requires addressing significant technical, ethical, and societal challenges. These include improving the safety, reliability, and longevity of implantable devices, ensuring privacy and security of neural data, and addressing concerns about autonomy, consent, and cognitive liberty.

Moreover, the integration of BCIs into everyday life raises complex questions about identity, agency, and the nature of consciousness. As BCIs become more advanced and pervasive, it is essential to engage in interdisciplinary dialogue and ethical reflection to ensure that these technologies serve the common good, uphold human rights, and respect human dignity.

Chapter 5

Humanoid Robots

Advancements in Robotics

The field of robotics has witnessed remarkable advancements in recent years, fueled by breakthroughs in artificial intelligence, materials science, and mechatronics. Among these innovations, humanoid robots stand out as one of the most captivating and promising developments, representing a convergence of cutting-edge technologies and human-like form factors.

Advancements in robotics have been driven by a combination of factors, including improvements in hardware capabilities, such as sensors, actuators, and power sources, as well as advances in software algorithms for perception, planning, and control. These advancements have enabled robots to perform increasingly complex tasks with greater autonomy, adaptability, and efficiency.

One of the key breakthroughs in robotics has been the development of anthropomorphic robots that mimic the physical appearance and capabilities of humans. These humanoid robots feature articulated limbs, dexterous hands, expressive faces, and sophisticated sensory systems, allowing them to interact with the world in a manner that closely resembles human behavior.

Moreover, advancements in artificial intelligence, particularly in the fields of machine learning and deep learning, have enabled robots to learn from experience, adapt to changing environments, and perform tasks that require perception, cognition, and decision-making. These AI-driven capabilities have expanded the range of applications for humanoid robots, from industrial automation and healthcare to entertainment and social interaction.

Applications and Use Cases

Humanoid robots have a wide range of applications across various industries and domains, each leveraging their unique capabilities to solve specific problems and address unmet needs.

In the field of healthcare, humanoid robots are being deployed to assist patients with activities of daily living, such as bathing, dressing, and medication reminders. These robots can provide physical assistance, emotional support, and companionship to elderly individuals, people with disabilities, or those recovering from injuries or surgeries. Moreover, humanoid robots can serve as telepresence devices, allowing healthcare providers to remotely monitor patients, conduct consultations, and deliver care services in real-time.

In the manufacturing sector, humanoid robots are being used for tasks that require dexterity, precision, and flexibility, such as assembly, inspection, and quality control. These robots can work alongside human workers in collaborative environments, performing repetitive or hazardous tasks while enhancing productivity, safety, and efficiency. Moreover, humanoid robots equipped with advanced sensors and AI algorithms can adapt to dynamic production environments, making them ideal for agile manufacturing processes.

In the field of education, humanoid robots are being employed as interactive tutors, mentors, and learning companions for students of all ages. These robots can deliver personalized instruction, facilitate collaborative learning activities, and provide feedback and encouragement to learners. Moreover, humanoid robots can serve as educational tools for teaching STEM subjects, programming, and robotics, inspiring curiosity, creativity, and critical thinking skills in students.

In the entertainment industry, humanoid robots are being used as performers, characters, and attractions in theme parks, museums, and entertainment venues. These robots can entertain audiences with music, dance, and storytelling, creating immersive and engaging experiences that captivate and delight spectators. Moreover, humanoid robots can interact with visitors, pose for photos, and provide information about exhibits or attractions, enhancing the overall entertainment value of the venue.

In the field of research and development, humanoid robots are being used as platforms for studying human-robot interaction, social robotics, and cognitive science. Researchers use humanoid robots to investigate topics such as emotion recognition, social cognition, and human-like behavior, gaining insights into the mechanisms underlying human intelligence and social interaction. Moreover, humanoid robots serve as testbeds for developing and evaluating algorithms for perception, planning, and control in complex and unstructured environments.

Future Trends in Robotics Development

Looking ahead, the future of humanoid robots is filled with exciting possibilities and transformative potential, driven by advances in technology, innovation, and collaboration.

One of the key trends in robotics development is the continued integration of artificial intelligence, machine learning, and computer vision techniques into humanoid robots. These AI-driven capabilities enable robots to perceive, understand, and interact with the world in more sophisticated and human-like ways, enhancing their autonomy, adaptability, and versatility.

Moreover, advancements in materials science, biomechanics, and human-robot interaction are enabling the development of more lifelike and expressive humanoid robots. These robots feature softer and more compliant materials, biomimetic designs, and human-inspired gestures and facial expressions, enhancing their ability to engage with humans in natural and intuitive ways.

Another trend in robotics development is the growing emphasis on social robotics and human-robot collaboration. As robots become more integrated into society and everyday life, there is a growing need for robots that can interact with humans in socially acceptable and culturally appropriate ways. These robots must be capable of understanding human intentions, emotions, and social cues, as well as adapting their behavior and communication style accordingly.

Furthermore, advancements in hardware miniaturization, power efficiency, and wireless communication are enabling the development of wearable and mobile robots that can assist humans in a wide range of tasks and environments. These robots can augment human capabilities, enhance productivity, and improve safety in fields such as healthcare, emergency response, and logistics.

In addition, there is growing interest in interdisciplinary research and collaboration to address the ethical, legal, and societal implications of humanoid robots. As robots become more integrated into society, there is a need to ensure that they are designed, deployed, and regulated in ways that promote human well-being, equity, and sustainability. This requires engaging stakeholders from diverse backgrounds, including policymakers, ethicists, social scientists, and the general public, in discussions about the ethical and societal implications of robotics.

Chapter 6

Generative AI

Understanding Generative AI

Generative Artificial Intelligence (AI) is a subfield of machine learning focused on creating models capable of generating new data samples that resemble a given dataset. Unlike traditional AI models that are designed for tasks like classification or regression, generative models aim to capture the underlying distribution of the data and generate new samples that are statistically similar to the training data.

One of the most popular approaches to generative AI is Generative Adversarial Networks (GANs), proposed by Ian Goodfellow and his colleagues in 2014. GANs consist of two neural networks: a generator and a discriminator. The generator generates fake data samples, while the discriminator evaluates whether a given sample is real or fake. Through a process of adversarial training, the generator learns to produce increasingly realistic samples, while the discriminator learns to distinguish between real and fake samples.

Another popular approach to generative AI is VariationalAutoencoders (VAEs), which are based on the principles of variational inference and autoencoder architecture. VAEs consist of an encoder network that maps input data to a latent space representation and a decoder network that generates output data samples from the latent space. By training the model to reconstruct input data samples while regularizing the distribution of the latent space, VAEs learn to generate new samples that resemble the training data.

Generative AI models have applications in a wide range of domains, including image and video generation, text-to-image synthesis, music composition, and drug discovery. These models enable researchers and practitioners to generate synthetic data samples for various purposes, such as data augmentation, content creation, and simulation.

Applications in Image and Video Generation

One of the most prominent applications of generative AI is in image and video generation, where models like GANs and VAEs have demonstrated remarkable capabilities in creating photorealistic images and videos from scratch.

In the realm of image generation, GANs have been used to generate high-resolution images of faces, animals, landscapes, and objects that are indistinguishable from real photographs. These models can learn to generate diverse and realistic images by capturing the underlying structure and variability of the training data. Moreover, GANs can be conditioned on additional information, such as class labels or textual descriptions, to generate images that meet specific criteria or constraints.

In addition to image generation, GANs and VAEs have been applied to the generation of videos, where they can create realistic sequences of frames that depict dynamic scenes and movements. These models can learn to generate coherent and smooth transitions between frames, enabling the creation of lifelike animations and visual effects.

Generative AI models have applications in various industries and domains, including entertainment, advertising, design, and virtual reality. These models can be used to create digital content, such as artwork, graphics, and animations, for use in video games, movies, and virtual environments. Moreover, generative AI can be used to generate personalized content for users, such as custom avatars, characters, or environments tailored to their preferences and interests.

Implications for Research and Innovation

Generative AI holds significant implications for research and innovation across various fields, offering new tools, techniques, and opportunities for exploration and discovery.

In the field of computer vision, generative AI models can be used for tasks such as image inpainting, super-resolution, and style transfer, where they can fill in missing parts of images, enhance image quality, or apply artistic styles to images, respectively. These capabilities have applications in fields such as image editing, restoration, and enhancement, enabling users to manipulate and transform images in novel and creative ways.

In the field of healthcare, generative AI models can be used to generate synthetic medical images, such as X-rays, MRI scans, or histopathology slides, for training and evaluation of diagnostic algorithms.

These models can generate diverse and realistic images that capture the variability and complexity of medical conditions, enabling researchers to develop and validate AI-based diagnostic tools that are robust and reliable.

In the field of design and creativity, generative AI models can be used to assist artists, designers, and creators in generating novel and inspiring content. These models can generate sketches, concepts, or prototypes based on input from users, providing inspiration and feedback to support the creative process. Moreover, generative AI can be used to explore new design spaces, generate alternative solutions, and push the boundaries of creativity and innovation.

In the field of education, generative AI models can be used to create educational content, such as interactive simulations, virtual laboratories, or digital tutors, that engage students and enhance learning outcomes. These models can generate personalized learning experiences tailored to individual students' needs, preferences, and learning styles, providing adaptive and interactive feedback to support their learning journey.

Chapter 7

Starlink Satellites and Internet

SpaceX'sStarlink Project

SpaceX'sStarlink project is a groundbreaking initiative aimed at providing global broadband internet coverage through a constellation of low Earth orbit (LEO) satellites. Founded by entrepreneur Elon Musk, SpaceX launched the first batch of Starlink satellites in May 2019, with plans to deploy thousands more in the coming years. The goal of the Starlink project is to bridge the digital divide by offering high-speed, low-latency internet access to underserved and remote areas around the world.

The Starlink constellation consists of small satellites orbiting the Earth at altitudes ranging from 340 to 1,200 kilometers. These satellites are interconnected through a network of ground stations and user terminals, enabling seamless communication between the satellites and end-user devices, such as smartphones, tablets, and computers. By distributing internet traffic across a large number of satellites, Starlink aims to provide reliable and high-performance internet service to users in even the most remote and inaccessible regions.

One of the key innovations of the Starlink project is the use of advanced satellite technology, including compact and lightweight satellites, phased array antennas, and optical inter-satellite links. These technologies enable Starlink satellites to communicate with each other and with ground stations using radio frequency (RF) signals and laser beams, providing high-speed data transmission and low-latency internet connectivity to users on the ground.

Moreover, SpaceX's reusable rocket technology allows for cost-effective and rapid deployment of Starlink satellites, with multiple satellite launches conducted on a single Falcon 9 rocket. This approach enables SpaceX to rapidly expand the Starlink constellation and scale up its internet service to reach millions of users worldwide.

Advantages and Challenges of Satellite Internet

Satellite internet offers several advantages compared to traditional terrestrial internet technologies, particularly in remote and underserved areas where access to high-speed broadband is limited or unavailable.

One of the primary advantages of satellite internet is its ability to provide coverage to geographically remote and isolated regions where laying fiber optic cables or building terrestrial infrastructure is impractical or cost-prohibitive. Satellite internet can reach users in rural areas, mountainous terrain, and maritime environments, enabling them to access the internet and connect with the global digital economy.

Moreover, satellite internet offers faster deployment and scalability compared to terrestrial infrastructure, allowing service providers to quickly expand coverage and capacity to meet growing demand. This flexibility is particularly valuable in disaster recovery scenarios, where satellite internet can provide emergency communication and connectivity in areas affected by natural disasters or infrastructure damage.

Furthermore, satellite internet offers low-latency connectivity for applications that require real-time communication and interaction, such as online gaming, video conferencing, and telemedicine. By leveraging advanced satellite technology and optimizing network architecture, satellite internet providers like Starlink can achieve latency comparable to or even better than traditional terrestrial internet services in certain scenarios.

However, satellite internet also poses several challenges and limitations that must be addressed to realize its full potential and ensure widespread adoption.

One of the main challenges of satellite internet is signal latency, which refers to the delay in data transmission caused by the time it takes for signals to travel between the satellite and the user's terminal. Although advances in satellite technology and network optimization have reduced latency in recent years, satellite internet still tends to have higher latency compared to terrestrial technologies like fiber optics and cable broadband. This latency can affect the performance of real-time applications and interactive services, leading to delays and disruptions in communication.

Another challenge of satellite internet is signal interference and degradation caused by atmospheric conditions, such as rain, snow, and fog, as well as electromagnetic interference from other sources, such as radio signals and electronic devices. These factors can affect the reliability and stability of satellite internet service, particularly in regions prone to adverse weather conditions or high levels of electromagnetic interference.

Moreover, satellite internet services typically have data caps and usage restrictions due to limited satellite bandwidth and capacity. This can result in slower speeds or additional fees for users who exceed their data allowances, leading to potential issues with affordability and accessibility, especially for users in rural or low-income areas.

Potential Impact on Global Connectivity

Despite these challenges, satellite internet has the potential to significantly impact global connectivity and bridge the digital divide by providing broadband access to underserved and remote regions around the world.

One of the key benefits of satellite internet is its ability to reach users in rural and isolated areas where traditional terrestrial infrastructure is lacking. By leveraging satellite technology, internet service providers can extend their coverage to regions that are currently underserved or unservedby terrestrial broadband networks, enabling users to access educational resources, healthcare services, and economic opportunities online.

Moreover, satellite internet can serve as a reliable backup and redundancy solution for terrestrial networks, providing resilience and continuity of service in the event of natural disasters, network outages, or infrastructure failures. This is particularly important in regions prone to extreme weather events, geological hazards, or political instability, where terrestrial infrastructure may be vulnerable or unreliable.

Furthermore, satellite internet can support a wide range of applications and use cases, including telemedicine, distance learning, precision agriculture, and e-commerce, that can contribute to economic development, social inclusion, and sustainable growth in underserved communities. By empowering individuals and businesses with high-speed internet access, satellite internet can unlock new opportunities for innovation, entrepreneurship, and collaboration across diverse sectors and industries.

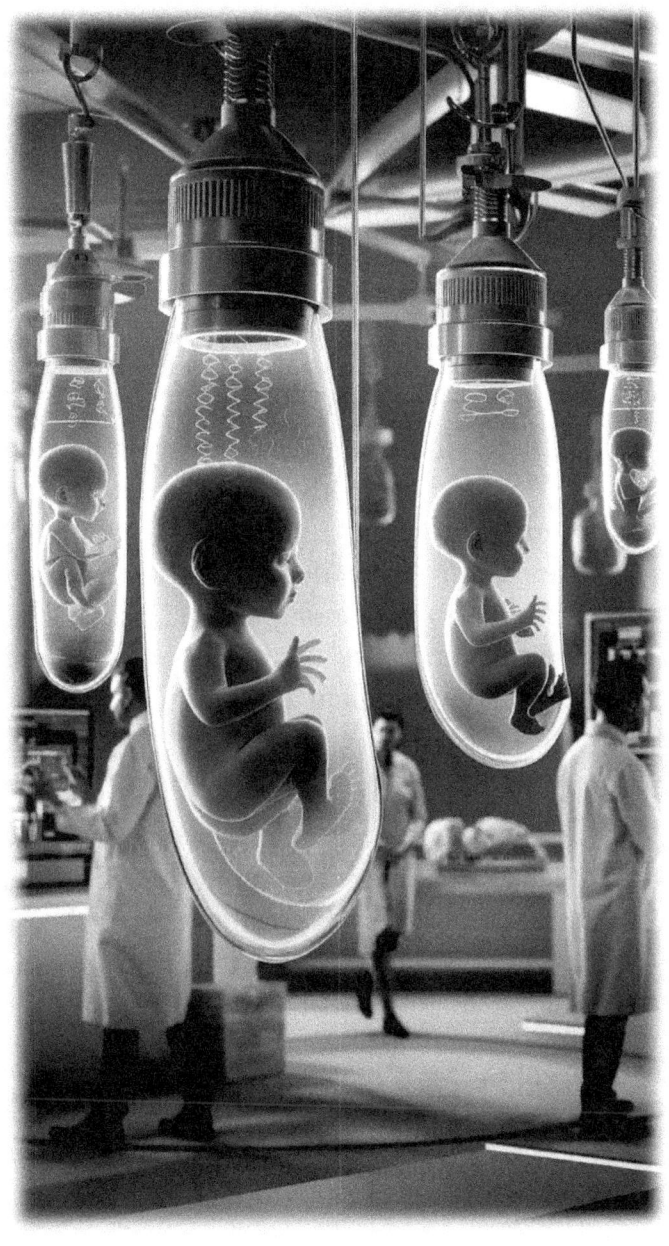

Chapter 8

Artificial Wombs

Concept and Current Research

Artificial wombs, also known as ectogenesis, refer to artificial environments that can support the development and growth of embryos or fetuses outside the mother's body. The concept of artificial wombs has been a topic of speculation and scientific inquiry for decades, with researchers exploring various technologies and approaches to replicate the conditions of the maternal womb and sustain fetal development ex vivo.

The development of artificial wombs holds the potential to revolutionize reproductive medicine and address numerous challenges and ethical dilemmas associated with traditional pregnancy and childbirth. By providing an alternative means of gestation outside the human body, artificial wombs could offer new opportunities for assisted reproduction, fetal therapy, and space exploration.

Current research on artificial wombs encompasses a wide range of disciplines, including bioengineering, biophysics, embryology, and neonatology. Researchers are investigating different strategies for creating artificial environments that can support embryonic and fetal development from conception to birth, mimicking the physiological conditions of the maternal womb as closely as possible.

One approach to artificial womb technology involves the use of bioreactors or incubators equipped with artificial amniotic fluid, temperature control systems, and nutrient delivery mechanisms. These bioreactors provide a controlled environment for growing embryos or fetuses, regulating factors such as oxygen levels, pH balance, and mechanical stimulation to support normal development.

Another approach to artificial womb technology involves the use of biomimetic scaffolds or matrices that mimic the structure and function of the maternal uterus. These scaffolds provide a three-dimensional framework for growing embryos or fetuses, facilitating nutrient exchange, waste removal, and tissue differentiation during gestation.

Moreover, advances in stem cell biology and tissue engineering are enabling researchers to create artificial placental tissues and organoids that can facilitate nutrient transfer and gas exchange between the maternal bloodstream and the developing fetus. These artificial placental models could serve as essential components of artificial womb systems, providing the necessary support for fetal growth and development.

While significant progress has been made in the development of artificial womb technology, numerous technical and ethical challenges remain to be addressed. These challenges include optimizing the design and functionality of artificial womb systems, ensuring the safety and efficacy of ex vivo gestation, and addressing ethical concerns related to embryo and fetal viability, autonomy, and personhood.

Potential Uses in Space Exploration and Human Reproduction

The potential applications of artificial wombs extend beyond terrestrial reproduction to include space exploration and colonization, where traditional pregnancy and childbirth are impractical or hazardous in the hostile environment of space.

In the context of space exploration, artificial wombs could enable astronauts to reproduce and raise offspring during long-duration missions or interplanetary voyages. By providing a safe and controlled environment for gestation and fetal development, artificial wombs could mitigate the risks and challenges associated with pregnancy and childbirth in microgravity or reduced-gravity environments.

Moreover, artificial wombs could support human reproduction in extraterrestrial habitats, such as lunar bases or Mars colonies, where environmental conditions are incompatible with traditional pregnancy and childbirth. By establishing self-contained ecosystems for gestation and fetal development, artificial wombs could enable humans to reproduce and sustain populations in space for extended periods.

Furthermore, artificial wombs could offer new options for assisted reproduction and fetal therapy on Earth, addressing infertility, pregnancy complications, and fetal anomalies that cannot be addressed by conventional means. By providing a controlled environment for gestation and fetal development, artificial wombs could offer hope to couples struggling with infertility or facing high-risk pregnancies, allowing them to conceive and carry a healthy baby to term.

In addition to medical applications, artificial wombs could have broader societal implications for reproductive rights, gender equality, and family planning. By shifting the locus of gestation from the maternal body to an artificial environment, artificial wombs could empower individuals to make informed choices about reproduction, pregnancy, and parenthood, free from the constraints of biological sex or reproductive biology.

Chapter 9

Nanotechnology

Introduction to Nanotechnology

Nanotechnology is a multidisciplinary field of science and engineering that deals with the manipulation and control of matter at the nanoscale, typically ranging from 1 to 100 nanometers. At this scale, materials exhibit unique properties and behaviors that differ from their bulk counterparts, enabling scientists and engineers to design and fabricate novel structures, devices, and systems with unprecedented precision and functionality.

The development of nanotechnology has led to numerous breakthroughs and innovations across various fields, including materials science, electronics, medicine, and environmental sustainability. By harnessing the principles of nanoscale physics and chemistry, researchers are able to engineer materials and devices with tailored properties and functionalities, offering new solutions to longstanding challenges and enabling new capabilities in science, technology, and industry.

Role of Nanotechnology in Various Fields

Nanotechnology plays a crucial role in advancing knowledge and innovation in a wide range of fields, including:

1. Materials Science: Nanotechnology enables the design and fabrication of advanced materials with tailored properties and functionalities, such as nanoparticles, nanocomposites, and nanostructured surfaces. These materials find applications in areas such as catalysis, energy storage, and structural materials, where their unique properties, such as high surface area, enhanced mechanical strength, and tunable optical properties, offer advantages over conventional materials.

2. Electronics and Photonics: Nanotechnology is driving advances in electronics and photonics by enabling the development of nanoscale devices and components, such as nanoscale transistors, quantum dots, and photonic crystals. These devices exhibit novel electronic and optical properties, such as enhanced conductivity, quantum confinement, and tunable emission spectra, which are essential for next-generation electronics, optoelectronics, and information technology.

3. Medicine and Healthcare: Nanotechnology has transformative potential in medicine and healthcare by enabling targeted drug delivery, diagnostic imaging, and regenerative medicine. Nanoparticle-based drug delivery systems can enhance the efficacy and reduce the side effects of therapeutic agents by targeting specific tissues or cells within the body. Nanoscale imaging probes and sensors offer high sensitivity and resolution for detecting disease biomarkers and monitoring biological processes in real-time. Moreover, nanomaterials can be used as scaffolds for tissue engineering and regenerative medicine, enabling the repair and regeneration of damaged tissues and organs.

4. Environmental Sustainability: Nanotechnology is driving innovations in environmental sustainability by enabling new approaches for pollution control, water purification, and renewable energy generation. Nanomaterials, such as carbon nanotubes, graphene, and nanoporous membranes, can be used for removing contaminants from air, water, and soil through processes such as adsorption, filtration, and catalysis. Nanotechnology also plays a role in developing advanced materials for energy storage and conversion, such as nanoscale batteries, supercapacitors, and photovoltaic cells, which are essential for transitioning to a sustainable energy future.

5. Agriculture and Food Technology: Nanotechnology offers opportunities for improving agricultural productivity, food safety, and nutritional quality. Nanoscale delivery systems can enhance the efficiency of agrochemicals, such as pesticides, fertilizers, and growth hormones, by targeting their release to specific plant tissues or soil environments. Nanosensors and biosensors can detect pathogens, toxins, and contaminants in food products, ensuring their safety and quality. Moreover, nanomaterials can be used for food packaging and preservation to extend the shelf life of perishable goods and reduce food waste.

Applications in Healthcare and Environmental Sustainability

Nanotechnology has numerous applications in healthcare and environmental sustainability, offering innovative solutions to address pressing challenges and improve quality of life.

1. Drug Delivery: Nanoparticle-based drug delivery systems enable targeted delivery of therapeutic agents to specific tissues or cells within the body, improving their efficacy and reducing their side effects. By encapsulating drugs within biocompatible nanoparticles, researchers can control their release kinetics, pharmacokinetics, and biodistribution, leading to improved therapeutic outcomes and patient compliance. Moreover, nanocarriers can overcome biological barriers, such as the blood-brain barrier, enabling the delivery of drugs to previously inaccessible sites for treating neurological disorders and cancers.

2. Diagnostic Imaging: Nanotechnology enables the development of advanced imaging probes and contrast agents for non-invasive detection and visualization of disease biomarkers and physiological processes in vivo. Nanoparticles, such as quantum dots, magnetic nanoparticles, and gold nanorods, offer unique optical, magnetic, and acoustic properties that can be exploited for various imaging modalities, including fluorescence imaging, magnetic resonance imaging (MRI), and photoacoustic imaging. These nanoprobes provide high sensitivity, resolution, and multiplexing capabilities for early detection, staging, and monitoring of diseases, such as cancer, cardiovascular disease, and neurodegenerative disorders.

3. Regenerative Medicine: Nanotechnology plays a vital role in regenerative medicine by providing biomaterials and scaffolds for tissue engineering and organ regeneration. Nanoscale materials, such as hydrogels, nanofibers, and nanoparticles, can mimic the extracellular matrix

(ECM) and provide structural support, mechanical cues, and biochemical signals to promote cell adhesion, proliferation, and differentiation. By engineering nanomaterials with specific properties, researchers can design scaffolds that guide the formation of functional tissues and organs, such as bone, cartilage, and blood vessels, for transplantation and regenerative therapies. Moreover, nanomaterials can be used for controlled release of growth factors, cytokines, and stem cells to enhance tissue regeneration and repair in vivo.

4. Environmental Remediation: Nanotechnology offers innovative solutions for environmental remediation by enabling the development of nanomaterial-based adsorbents, catalysts, and sensors for pollutant removal, energy conversion, and monitoring of environmental contaminants. Nanoporous materials, such as activated carbon, zeolites, and metal-organic frameworks (MOFs), exhibit high surface area, porosity, and adsorption capacity for capturing and sequestering pollutants from air, water, and soil. Nanocatalysts, such as metal nanoparticles and metal oxide nanomaterials, can catalyze chemical reactions for decomposing hazardous compounds, degrading organic pollutants, and converting toxic gases into non-toxic byproducts. Moreover, nanosensors and biosensors offer sensitive and selective detection of environmental contaminants, such as heavy metals, pesticides, and pathogens, enabling real-time monitoring and assessment of environmental quality.

Chapter 10

Internet of Things (IoT)

Overview of IoT Technology

The Internet of Things (IoT) is a transformative technology paradigm that connects everyday objects and devices to the internet, enabling them to communicate, collect data, and perform intelligent actions autonomously. IoT technology encompasses a wide range of devices, sensors, and systems embedded with connectivity, computing, and sensing capabilities, which enable them to interact with their environment, exchange information, and execute tasks without human intervention.

At the heart of IoT technology are sensors and actuators that collect data from the physical world and actuate changes in response to commands or triggers. These sensors can measure various parameters, such as temperature, humidity, pressure, motion, and light, providing real-time insights into the state and behavior of objects and environments. Actuators, on the other hand, can control physical processes or devices based on input from sensors, enabling remote monitoring and control of connected systems.

IoT devices are typically connected to the internet via wired or wireless networks, such as Wi-Fi, Bluetooth, Zigbee, or cellular networks, which allow them to communicate with each other, cloud platforms, and user interfaces. Cloud computing plays a crucial role in IoT deployments by providing scalable storage, processing, and analytics capabilities for managing large volumes of data generated by IoT devices and applications. Cloud-based IoT platforms enable organizations to collect, store, analyze, and visualize data from diverse sources, facilitating insights and decision-making in real-time.

Moreover, IoT technology leverages advanced technologies such as artificial intelligence (AI), machine learning (ML), and edge computing to enable intelligent automation, predictive analytics, and adaptive control in IoT applications. AI and ML algorithms can analyze sensor data, detect patterns, and make predictions or recommendations based on historical data, enabling proactive maintenance, anomaly detection, and optimization in IoT systems. Edge computing, on the other hand, allows data processing and decision-making to be performed closer to the source of data generation, reducing latency, bandwidth usage, and reliance on centralized cloud infrastructure.

The proliferation of IoT technology is driving digital transformation across various industries, including manufacturing, healthcare, transportation, agriculture, smart cities, and consumer electronics. IoT-enabled solutions are unlocking new opportunities for innovation, efficiency, and sustainability by enabling smarter, more connected, and autonomous systems.

Smart Cities and Healthcare Applications

1. Smart Cities:

Smart cities represent one of the most promising applications of IoT technology, aiming to enhance urban infrastructure, services, and quality of life through data-driven insights and automation. IoT-enabled smart city solutions leverage sensors, cameras, and actuators deployed across urban areas to collect data on traffic, energy consumption, air quality, waste management, public safety, and infrastructure usage. This data is then analyzed in real-time to optimize resource allocation, improve service delivery, and enhance urban resilience.

Traffic management is one of the key areas where IoT technology is making a significant impact in smart cities. IoT-enabled traffic sensors and cameras installed on roads, intersections, and public transit systems collect data on traffic flow, congestion, and accidents in real-time. This data is used to optimize traffic signal timing, reroute vehicles, and manage congestion dynamically, reducing travel times, fuel consumption, and carbon emissions. Moreover, IoT-enabled smart parking systems utilize sensors and mobile apps to guide drivers to available parking spaces, reducing traffic congestion and emissions caused by circling for parking.

Energy management is another critical application of IoT technology in smart cities, aiming to optimize energy consumption, reduce greenhouse gas emissions, and improve energy efficiency. IoT-enabled smart grids and meters collect data on electricity usage, demand patterns, and grid performance, enabling utilities to monitor, manage, and optimize energy distribution in real-time. By analyzing this data, utilities can identify inefficiencies, detect faults, and implement demand response programs to balance supply and demand, reduce peak loads, and enhance grid stability.

Furthermore, IoT technology is revolutionizing public safety and security in smart cities by enabling real-time monitoring, surveillance, and emergency response. IoT-enabled surveillance cameras, acoustic sensors, and gunshot detectors installed in public spaces, transportation hubs, and critical infrastructure monitor for security threats, unauthorized activities, and emergencies. This data is analyzed using AI-powered video analytics and pattern recognition algorithms to identify suspicious behavior, trigger alerts, and dispatch first responders promptly. Moreover, IoT-enabled emergency response systems leverage geolocation data from mobile devices and wearables to locate and assist individuals in distress, improving emergency response times and outcomes.

Overall, IoT technology is transforming urban environments into smarter, more efficient, and sustainable cities by enabling data-driven decision-making, automation, and optimization across various domains, including transportation, energy, public safety, and governance. As the deployment of IoT-enabled smart city solutions continues to expand, the potential for innovation and improvement in urban living standards is vast.

2. Healthcare Applications:

IoT technology is revolutionizing healthcare by enabling remote patient monitoring, personalized medicine, and predictive analytics, leading to improved patient outcomes, reduced healthcare costs, and enhanced quality of care. IoT-enabled healthcare solutions leverage wearable devices, medical sensors, and telehealth platforms to collect patient data, monitor vital signs, and deliver personalized interventions in real-time.

Remote patient monitoring (RPM) is a key application of IoT technology in healthcare, allowing healthcare providers to monitor patients' health status and adherence to treatment plans outside traditional clinical settings. IoT-enabled wearable devices, such as smartwatches, fitness trackers, and medical sensors, collect data on vital signs, physical activity, and sleep patterns continuously. This data is transmitted to healthcare providers via secure networks, allowing them to track patients' progress, detect early signs of deterioration, and intervene proactively to prevent adverse events. RPM is particularly valuable for managing chronic conditions, such as diabetes, hypertension, and heart disease, by enabling early intervention, reducing hospitalizations, and improving patient outcomes.

Personalized medicine is another area where IoT technology is driving innovation in healthcare, aiming to deliver tailored treatments and interventions based on individual patients' genetic, physiological, and lifestyle characteristics. IoT-enabled medical devices, such as genetic sequencers, biosensors, and implantable devices, generate large volumes of data on patients' biomarkers, genetic variants, and treatment responses. This data is analyzed using AI and ML algorithms to identify patterns, correlations, and predictive models that inform personalized treatment plans, drug dosages, and lifestyle recommendations. By delivering targeted therapies and interventions, personalized medicine holds the potential to improve treatment efficacy, minimize side effects, and optimize patient outcomes.

Predictive analytics is also transforming healthcare by leveraging IoT-generated data to forecast disease outbreaks, identify high-risk patients, and optimize healthcare resource allocation. IoT-enabled healthcare systems collect data from diverse sources, such as electronic health records, medical devices, and population health databases, to build predictive models that anticipate health trends, patient outcomes, and healthcare utilization patterns. These models enable healthcare providers to identify at-risk populations, allocate resources efficiently, and implement preventive interventions proactively, reducing healthcare costs and improving population health outcomes.

Moreover, IoT technology is facilitating the shift towards patient-centric care models, empowering patients to take an active role in managing their health and well-being. IoT-enabled patient portals, mobile apps, and telehealth platforms provide patients with access to their health data, educational resources, and remote consultations with healthcare providers. By enabling continuous monitoring, self-management, and virtual care delivery, IoT technology enhances patients' engagement, adherence to treatment regimens, and overall satisfaction with healthcare services.

Chapter 11

Autonomous Vehicles

Advancements in Self-Driving Technology

Autonomous vehicles (AVs), also known as self-driving cars or driverless vehicles, represent a transformative technology that has the potential to revolutionize transportation systems and urban mobility. AVs are equipped with sensors, cameras, radars, and advanced computing systems that enable them to perceive their surroundings, interpret road conditions, and navigate safely without human intervention.

The development of self-driving technology has been driven by advancements in artificial intelligence (AI), machine learning (ML), sensor technology, and high-performance computing. AI algorithms enable AVs to analyze sensor data, recognize objects, and make real-time decisions in complex driving scenarios. ML algorithms allow AVs to learn from experience and improve their performance over time, enabling them to adapt to changing environments and unforeseen situations.

One of the key advancements in self-driving technology is the development of perception systems that enable AVs to accurately detect and classify objects in their vicinity. LiDAR (Light Detection and Ranging) sensors use laser beams to create detailed 3D maps of the surrounding environment, allowing AVs to identify obstacles, pedestrians, cyclists, and other vehicles with high precision. Radar sensors detect objects based on radio waves, while cameras capture visual information, such as traffic signs, lane markings, and traffic lights. These sensor technologies work together to provide redundant and complementary information, ensuring robust perception capabilities in diverse driving conditions.

Another critical advancement in self-driving technology is the development of decision-making algorithms that enable AVs to plan safe and efficient trajectories in real-time. AVs use probabilistic models, optimization techniques, and rule-based algorithms to analyze sensor data, predict the behavior of other road users, and plan collision-free paths to their destinations. These decision-making algorithms consider factors such as traffic flow, road geometry, speed limits, and traffic regulations to ensure smooth and lawful operation in various driving scenarios.

Furthermore, advancements in vehicle-to-everything (V2X) communication technology enable AVs to exchange information with other vehicles, infrastructure, and traffic management systems in real-time. V2X communication allows AVs to share information about their location, speed, trajectory, and intentions with nearby vehicles, enabling cooperative driving behaviors, such as platooning, merging, and intersection negotiation. Moreover, V2X communication enables AVs to receive real-time updates about road conditions, traffic congestion, and road closures, allowing them to adapt their routes dynamically and avoid potential hazards or delays.

The development of simulation and testing platforms has also been instrumental in advancing self-driving technology by enabling rigorous validation and verification of AVs in virtual environments. Simulation platforms allow researchers and engineers to simulate millions of miles of driving scenarios, including rare and dangerous situations, in a safe and controlled manner. This enables AV developers to test and refine their algorithms, sensor systems, and control strategies under a wide range of conditions, ensuring the safety and reliability of AVs before they are deployed on public roads.

Overall, the advancements in self-driving technology have brought AVs closer to commercialization and widespread adoption, with numerous companies and research institutions investing heavily in AV research and development. While significant challenges remain, such as regulatory approval, public acceptance, and technical reliability, the progress made in recent years has positioned AVs as a promising solution to improve road safety, reduce congestion, and enhance mobility for all.

Impact on Transportation and Logistics

The widespread adoption of autonomous vehicles (AVs) is expected to have profound impacts on transportation systems, urban mobility, and logistics operations. AVs promise to improve road safety, reduce traffic congestion, and enhance mobility by enabling efficient, convenient, and accessible transportation services for individuals and goods.

One of the key impacts of AVs on transportation is the potential to improve road safety by reducing human errors, which are responsible for the majority of traffic accidents. AVs are equipped with advanced sensors, cameras, and computing systems that enable them to perceive their surroundings, anticipate hazards, and react quickly to changing road conditions. By eliminating human errors such as speeding, distraction, and impairment, AVs have the potential to significantly reduce the number of accidents, injuries, and fatalities on our roads, making transportation safer for everyone.

Moreover, AVs have the potential to reduce traffic congestion and improve traffic flow by optimizing vehicle trajectories, reducing unnecessary stops and delays, and enabling smoother and more efficient traffic patterns. AVs can communicate with each other and with traffic management systems in real-time, allowing them to coordinate their movements, merge lanes, and navigate intersections more efficiently. By reducing congestion and improving traffic flow, AVs can reduce travel times, fuel consumption, and emissions, leading to environmental benefits and economic savings for society.

Furthermore, AVs have the potential to transform urban mobility by providing convenient, accessible, and affordable transportation options for individuals and communities. Shared AV services, such as ride-hailing, car-sharing, and micro-transit, can provide on-demand transportation services that complement existing public transit systems and fill gaps in underserved areas. AVs can also enable new mobility solutions for populations with limited mobility, such as seniors, people with disabilities, and residents of rural areas, by providing door-to-door transportation services that are accessible, safe, and reliable.

In addition to passenger transportation, AVs have the potential to revolutionize logistics operations by enabling autonomous delivery vehicles and drones that can transport goods efficiently and cost-effectively. AVs can be deployed in last-mile delivery operations, warehouse logistics, and freight transportation, enabling retailers, e-commerce companies, and logistics providers to optimize their supply chain operations, reduce delivery times, and lower costs. Autonomous delivery vehicles can navigate urban environments, deliver packages to customers' doorsteps, and return to distribution centers autonomously, reducing the need for human drivers and improving the efficiency of delivery operations.

Chapter 12

Space Tourism

Current State and Future Prospects

Space tourism, once a futuristic concept, is now becoming a reality, with several companies actively working to make commercial space travel accessible to private individuals. While space tourism is still in its infancy, recent advancements in space technology, the emergence of private spaceflight companies, and increasing public interest in space exploration have fueled the growth of the space tourism industry.

The current state of space tourism is characterized by a small but growing number of suborbital and orbital spaceflight missions offered by private spaceflight companies such as SpaceX, Blue Origin, and Virgin Galactic. These companies are developing spacecraft and launch vehicles capable of carrying paying passengers on short-duration spaceflights, offering them the opportunity to experience weightlessness, see the curvature of the Earth, and witness breathtaking views of space.

Suborbital space tourism missions involve brief flights to the edge of space, typically reaching altitudes of around 100 kilometers above the Earth's surface. Passengers experience a few minutes of weightlessness before returning to Earth, providing them with a taste of space travel without the need for extensive training or orbital mechanics knowledge. Companies like Blue Origin and Virgin Galactic are developing reusable suborbital spacecraft, such as New Shepard and SpaceShipTwo, respectively, to offer commercial suborbital space tourism flights to paying customers in the near future.

On the other hand, orbital space tourism missions involve longer-duration flights to low Earth orbit (LEO), where passengers spend several days aboard a spacecraft orbiting the Earth. These missions offer a more immersive space travel experience, allowing passengers to live and work in space, conduct scientific experiments, and observe the Earth from a unique vantage point. SpaceX's Crew Dragon spacecraft, which has been used to transport astronauts to the International Space Station (ISS), is expected to be used for commercial orbital space tourism missions in the coming years, with plans to offer private crewed missions to LEO for individuals, corporations, and research organizations.

While space tourism is still primarily limited to wealthy individuals and celebrities due to its high cost, there is growing interest and investment in making space travel more accessible and affordable to a broader audience. Companies like SpaceX and Blue Origin are working to reduce the cost of space access through the development of reusable launch vehicles and spacecraft, which can significantly lower the price of space tourism flights over time. Additionally, advances in space infrastructure, such as space hotels, orbital habitats, and space stations, could enable longer-duration space tourism missions and accommodate larger numbers of passengers in the future.

Moreover, the emergence of space tourism as a commercial industry has sparked competition and innovation among spaceflight companies, leading to the development of new technologies, business models, and partnerships in the space sector. Companies like SpaceX, Blue Origin, and Virgin Galactic are vying for market share in the space tourism industry by offering unique experiences, competitive pricing, and reliable launch services to customers. As the industry matures and competition intensifies, we can expect to see continued advancements in space tourism technology, increased accessibility, and a wider range of options for prospective space tourists.

Looking ahead, the future of space tourism holds great promise, with the potential to revolutionize the way we travel, explore, and experience the cosmos. As technology continues to evolve, and spaceflight becomes more accessible and affordable, we may see a dramatic increase in the number of people traveling to space for leisure, adventure, research, and business purposes. From suborbital joyrides to orbital vacations and beyond, space tourism offers a glimpse into a future where the final frontier is open to all who dare to dream of reaching for the stars.

Orbital Flights and Extended Space Travel

Orbital flights and extended space travel represent the next frontier in space tourism, offering passengers the opportunity to venture beyond Earth's atmosphere and experience the wonders of space for longer durations. While suborbital space tourism provides a brief taste of weightlessness and spaceflight, orbital flights and extended space travel missions offer a more immersive and transformative experience, allowing passengers to live and work in space for days, weeks, or even months at a time.

Orbital space tourism missions involve launching passengers aboard a spacecraft into low Earth orbit (LEO), where they spend several days aboard a space station or orbital habitat, conducting scientific experiments, performing spacewalks, and observing the Earth from a unique vantage point. The International Space Station (ISS) has served as a destination for government astronauts and space tourists alike, hosting visitors from various countries and space agencies over the years. In recent years, private spaceflight companies like SpaceX have announced plans to offer commercial orbital space tourism missions to LEO, using their crewed spacecraft to transport paying passengers to and from the ISS.

Extended space travel missions, on the other hand, involve journeys beyond LEO to destinations such as the Moon, Mars, or beyond. While no commercial extended space tourism missions have been launched yet, there is growing interest and investment in sending private individuals on deep space missions in the future. Companies like SpaceX, Blue Origin, and NASA are developing spacecraft and launch vehicles capable of carrying passengers to the Moon and beyond, with plans to offer commercial lunar tourism missions, circumlunar flights, and missions to Mars in the coming decades.

One of the key challenges of orbital flights and extended space travel missions is ensuring the safety, comfort, and well-being of passengers during their journey in space. Spacecraft and habitats must be equipped with life support systems, radiation shielding, and environmental controls to provide a habitable and safe living environment for passengers in space. Additionally, passengers must undergo rigorous training and medical screening to prepare them for the physical and psychological challenges of space travel, including microgravity, radiation exposure, and isolation.

Furthermore, the economic viability of orbital flights and extended space travel missions depends on factors such as launch costs, spacecraft reliability, and market demand for space tourism. While the cost of space travel is still prohibitively high for most people, advances in space technology, economies of scale, and competition among spaceflight companies are expected to drive down the cost of space tourism over time, making it more accessible and affordable to a broader audience.

Chapter 13

Smart Cities

Role of IoT and Data Analytics

Smart cities represent a paradigm shift in urban development and management, leveraging the power of digital technologies to improve the efficiency, sustainability, and livability of urban environments. At the heart of smart cities are interconnected networks of Internet of Things (IoT) devices, sensors, and data analytics platforms that collect, analyze, and act upon real-time data to optimize city operations, enhance service delivery, and empower citizens.

The Internet of Things (IoT) plays a central role in smart cities by connecting physical objects, infrastructure, and systems to the internet, enabling them to communicate, interact, and share data with each other autonomously. IoT devices, such as sensors, actuators, and smart meters, are deployed throughout the city to monitor environmental conditions, infrastructure assets, and public services in real-time. These devices collect a wealth of data on various aspects of urban life, including air quality, traffic flow, energy consumption, waste management, and public safety, providing valuable insights into city dynamics and performance.

Data analytics is another key component of smart cities, enabling city planners, policymakers, and administrators to make informed decisions and optimize city operations based on data-driven insights. Advanced analytics techniques, such as machine learning, artificial intelligence, and predictive modeling, are used to analyze large volumes of data collected from IoT devices and other sources, identify patterns, trends, and anomalies, and generate actionable recommendations for improving urban efficiency and sustainability.

By harnessing the power of IoT and data analytics, smart cities can achieve a wide range of benefits across various domains, including transportation, energy, healthcare, public safety, and environmental sustainability. In transportation, for example, IoT-enabled traffic management systems can monitor traffic flow in real-time, optimize traffic signal timings, and provide dynamic routing recommendations to reduce congestion and improve travel times. In energy, smart grids and meters can optimize energy distribution, detect and respond to power outages, and encourage energy conservation among residents and businesses.

Moreover, IoT devices and data analytics platforms can enhance public safety and emergency response capabilities by providing real-time monitoring of crime patterns, natural disasters, and public health emergencies. Smart surveillance systems, for instance, can detect and alert authorities to suspicious activities or incidents, while predictive analytics models can anticipate and mitigate the impact of disasters before they occur. In healthcare, IoT-enabled telemedicine solutions can enable remote monitoring of patients' health status, facilitate virtual consultations, and improve access to healthcare services in underserved areas.

Improving Urban Living and Sustainability:

One of the primary goals of smart cities is to improve the quality of life for residents by creating safer, healthier, and more sustainable urban environments. By leveraging IoT and data analytics technologies, smart cities can address key challenges facing modern cities, such as traffic congestion, air pollution, energy consumption, and waste management, while enhancing urban livability and resilience.

In transportation, smart cities can reduce traffic congestion and improve air quality by promoting the use of public transit, cycling, and shared mobility services. Real-time traffic monitoring and congestion pricing schemes can incentivize behavior change and encourage residents to use alternative modes of transportation, reducing the reliance on private cars and mitigating the environmental impact of traffic congestion. Additionally, smart parking systems can optimize parking availability and pricing, reducing the time spent searching for parking spaces and alleviating traffic congestion in urban areas.

Furthermore, smart cities can promote energy efficiency and sustainability by deploying IoT-enabled energy management systems, renewable energy sources, and energy-efficient building technologies. Smart grids and meters can monitor and optimize energy consumption in real-time, enabling demand-response programs and time-of-use pricing strategies to encourage energy conservation and reduce peak demand. Renewable energy sources, such as solar panels and wind turbines, can generate clean and sustainable energy to power urban infrastructure and reduce reliance on fossil fuels.

Moreover, smart cities can enhance environmental sustainability and resilience by implementing IoT-enabled waste management systems, water conservation measures, and green infrastructure solutions. Smart waste bins equipped with sensors can monitor waste levels and optimize collection routes, reducing fuel consumption and emissions associated with waste collection. Water conservation measures, such as smart irrigation systems and leak detection sensors, can optimize water usage and reduce water waste in urban landscapes. Green infrastructure, such as green roofs, rain gardens, and permeable pavements, can mitigate the effects of urban heat islands, reduce stormwater runoff, and improve air quality in urban areas.

Chapter 14

Mixed Reality

Applications in Various Industries

Mixed reality (MR) is a cutting-edge technology that blends elements of both virtual reality (VR) and augmented reality (AR) to create immersive, interactive experiences that seamlessly integrate digital content into the physical world. MR applications span a wide range of industries and domains, from entertainment and gaming to healthcare, education, manufacturing, and beyond. By combining the virtual and physical worlds in real-time, mixed reality has the potential to revolutionize how we work, play, learn, and interact with the world around us.

In entertainment and gaming, mixed reality offers immersive experiences that blur the line between fantasy and reality, allowing users to engage with digital content in new and exciting ways. Mixed reality gaming platforms, such as Microsoft's HoloLens and Magic Leap's Magic Leap One, enable users to interact with virtual characters, objects, and environments overlaid onto the real world. Whether it's battling virtual monsters in your living room or exploring fantastical worlds in your backyard, mixed reality gaming offers endless possibilities for entertainment and escapism.

Moreover, mixed reality has applications beyond entertainment, with significant potential to transform industries such as healthcare, where it can be used for medical training, surgical planning, patient education, and remote consultations. Mixed reality simulations enable medical students and professionals to practice procedures in a realistic, risk-free environment, improving their skills and confidence before performing surgeries on real patients. Surgeons can use mixed reality to visualize patient anatomy in 3D, plan surgical procedures more effectively, and navigate complex surgical environments with greater precision and accuracy.

In education, mixed reality offers immersive learning experiences that engage students and enhance their understanding of complex concepts. Mixed reality simulations can transport students to virtual environments, such as historical landmarks, scientific phenomena, or outer space, allowing them to explore and interact with educational content in a hands-on, experiential way. For example, students can take a virtual field trip to ancient Rome, witness the formation of a tornado, or dissect a virtual frog, all from the comfort of their classroom.

Furthermore, mixed reality has applications in manufacturing and engineering, where it can be used for product design, prototyping, assembly, and maintenance. Mixed reality tools, such as Microsoft's Dynamics 365 Remote Assist and Guides, enable workers to access digital instructions, schematics, and overlays overlaid onto physical objects in real-time, improving productivity, efficiency, and safety on the factory floor. Engineers can use mixed reality to visualize and manipulate 3D CAD models, simulate assembly processes, and identify potential design flaws before production begins.

Additionally, mixed reality has potential applications in retail and marketing, where it can be used to create immersive shopping experiences, virtual showrooms, and interactive product demonstrations. Retailers can use mixed reality to visualize and customize products in real-time, allowing customers to preview furniture in their homes, try on virtual clothes, or test drive virtual cars before making a purchase. Mixed reality marketing campaigns can engage consumers with interactive experiences that showcase products and services in innovative and memorable ways, driving brand awareness and customer engagement.

Future Trends and Potential Developments

Looking ahead, the future of mixed reality holds tremendous potential for innovation and growth, with a wide range of emerging trends and developments shaping the evolution of the technology across various industries.

One of the key trends in mixed reality is the convergence of VR, AR, and MR technologies into unified platforms that offer seamless transitions between virtual, augmented, and mixed reality experiences. Companies like Meta (formerly Facebook) and Apple are investing heavily in the development of all-in-one mixed reality headsets that combine the best elements of VR and AR into versatile devices capable of delivering immersive experiences across a wide range of applications.

Moreover, advancements in hardware technology, such as improved display resolution, field of view, and tracking accuracy, are enabling more immersive and realistic mixed reality experiences with greater fidelity and presence. Future mixed reality headsets are expected to offer higher resolution displays, wider field of view, and more accurate positional tracking, allowing users to see and interact with virtual content with unprecedented clarity and realism.

Furthermore, the integration of artificial intelligence (AI) and machine learning (ML) algorithms into mixed reality applications is enabling new capabilities, such as real-time object recognition, scene understanding, and natural language processing. AI-powered mixed reality experiences can adapt to user preferences, personalize content, and anticipate user needs, creating more engaging and immersive interactions that feel natural and intuitive.

Additionally, the proliferation of 5G networks and edge computing infrastructure is expected to accelerate the adoption of mixed reality by enabling low-latency, high-bandwidth connectivity that is essential for streaming immersive content and processing complex simulations in real-time. 5G-enabled mixed reality applications can deliver high-quality, interactive experiences to users anywhere, anytime, without the need for expensive hardware or extensive computational resources.

Moreover, the rise of the metaverse, a collective virtual shared space that is created by the convergence of physical and digital worlds, is expected to drive demand for mixed reality experiences that enable users to socialize, collaborate, and create together in immersive virtual environments. Companies like Roblox, Fortnite, and Decentraland are pioneering the development of metaverse platforms that offer users unprecedented freedom and creativity to explore and interact with virtual worlds in ways that were previously unimaginable.

Furthermore, the democratization of mixed reality development tools and platforms is empowering creators, developers, and businesses to build their own mixed reality experiences without the need for specialized technical expertise or resources. User-friendly development platforms, such as Unity, Unreal Engine, and Microsoft Mixed Reality Toolkit, provide developers with powerful tools and libraries for creating immersive content, designing interactive experiences, and deploying applications across multiple devices and platforms.

Chapter 15

3D Printing

Overview of 3D Printing Technology

3D printing, also known as additive manufacturing, is a revolutionary technology that enables the creation of three-dimensional objects by layering materials, typically plastic, metal, or ceramic, based on digital 3D models. Unlike traditional manufacturing methods, which involve subtractive processes like cutting or molding, 3D printing builds objects layer by layer from the bottom up, allowing for greater design flexibility, customization, and complexity.

The process of 3D printing begins with the creation of a digital 3D model using computer-aided design (CAD) software or by scanning an existing object using 3D scanning technology. The digital model is then sliced into thin horizontal layers using slicing software, which generates a set of instructions, known as G-code, that directs the 3D printer to deposit material layer by layer according to the design specifications.

There are several types of 3D printing technologies, each with its own unique process and materials. The most common types of 3D printing technologies include:

1. Fused Deposition Modeling (FDM): FDM is one of the most widely used 3D printing technologies, where thermoplastic filaments are heated to their melting point and extruded through a nozzle onto a build platform, where they cool and solidify to form layers. FDM is known for its versatility, affordability, and ease of use, making it ideal for rapid prototyping, product development, and hobbyist applications.

2. Stereolithography (SLA): SLA uses a liquid photopolymer resin that is cured, or hardened, by exposure to ultraviolet (UV) light layer by layer to create objects with high levels of detail and accuracy. SLA is commonly used in industries such as jewelry, dentistry, and automotive manufacturing, where precision and surface finish are critical.

3. Selective Laser Sintering (SLS): SLS employs a high-powered laser to selectively sinter, or fuse together, powdered materials, such as nylon, metal, or ceramic, layer by layer to create complex 3D objects. SLS is known for its ability to produce durable, functional parts with high strength and heat resistance, making it suitable for aerospace, medical, and industrial applications.

4. Direct Metal Laser Sintering (DMLS): DMLS is a variation of SLS that uses a high-powered laser to selectively sinter metal powders, such as titanium, aluminum, or stainless steel, layer by layer to create metal parts with complex geometries and excellent mechanical properties. DMLS is used in aerospace, automotive, and medical industries for producing high-performance components with tight tolerances.

5. Binder Jetting: Binder jetting involves depositing a liquid binding agent onto a powder bed of material, such as sand, ceramic, or metal, layer by layer to bind the particles together and form solid objects. Binder jetting is used for producing sand molds and cores for metal casting, as well as metal and ceramic parts for aerospace, automotive, and consumer goods applications.

Advancements in 3D printing technology have led to the development of new materials, processes, and applications that are pushing the boundaries of what is possible with additive manufacturing. Researchers and engineers are exploring novel techniques, such as multi-material 3D printing, bioprinting, and 4D printing, to create functional prototypes, custom medical implants, and even living tissue and organs.

Advancements and Novel Applications

One of the most significant advancements in 3D printing technology is the development of multi-material printing capabilities, which enable the simultaneous deposition of multiple materials to create objects with varying mechanical, electrical, or optical properties. Multi-material 3D printing is revolutionizing industries such as aerospace, where lightweight, multifunctional parts can be produced with integrated sensors, electronics, and actuators for aircraft and spacecraft applications.

Moreover, bioprinting is a rapidly emerging field within 3D printing that involves the deposition of living cells and biomaterials to create tissue-engineered constructs for regenerative medicine, drug testing, and organ transplantation. Bioprinting techniques enable researchers to fabricate complex 3D structures, such as blood vessels, heart valves, and skin grafts, using patient-specific cells and biomaterials, offering new possibilities for personalized medicine and tissue regeneration.

Another groundbreaking advancement in 3D printing technology is 4D printing, which involves the use of smart materials that can change shape, structure, or function in response to external stimuli, such as temperature, humidity, or light, over time. 4D printing enables the fabrication of dynamic, self-assembling structures that can adapt to their environment, fold, twist, or unfold autonomously, offering new opportunities for responsive architecture, soft robotics, and adaptive materials.

Furthermore, the adoption of 3D printing in mainstream manufacturing is accelerating, driven by advancements in materials, processes, and cost-effective solutions that are making additive manufacturing more accessible and scalable for mass production. Companies are leveraging 3D printing for rapid prototyping, tooling, jigs, fixtures, and end-use parts across a wide range of industries, including automotive, aerospace, healthcare, and consumer goods.

Additionally, the rise of distributed manufacturing and on-demand production models is transforming the way products are designed, manufactured, and distributed, with 3D printing playing a central role in enabling decentralized, localized production networks. Digital manufacturing platforms, such as 3D Hubs and Shapeways, connect designers, manufacturers, and consumers in a global marketplace where custom products can be produced on demand, reducing inventory, waste, and transportation costs.

Chapter 16

Fusion Power

Promise of Clean and Limitless Energy

Fusion power holds the promise of providing clean, safe, and virtually limitless energy by harnessing the same process that powers the sun and other stars: nuclear fusion. Unlike nuclear fission, which involves splitting atoms to release energy, nuclear fusion involves fusing atomic nuclei together to form heavier elements, releasing a tremendous amount of energy in the process.

At the core of fusion power is the fusion of isotopes of hydrogen, particularly deuterium and tritium, under conditions of extreme temperature and pressure. When deuterium and tritium nuclei fuse together, they form a helium nucleus and release a neutron, along with a vast amount of energy in the form of heat and radiation. This process, known as thermonuclear fusion, has the potential to generate immense amounts of energy from relatively small amounts of fuel, with no greenhouse gas emissions or long-lived radioactive waste.

One of the primary advantages of fusion power is its abundance of fuel sources. Deuterium, a stable isotope of hydrogen, can be extracted from seawater or produced from lithium, which is plentiful in the Earth's crust. Tritium, while not naturally abundant, can be bred from lithium within a fusion reactor itself, ensuring a virtually limitless supply of fuel for fusion power plants. As a result, fusion power has the potential to provide energy security and independence from fossil fuels, reducing reliance on finite and environmentally harmful resources.

Moreover, fusion power offers significant environmental benefits compared to conventional energy sources, such as coal, oil, and natural gas. Fusion reactions produce no greenhouse gas emissions, such as carbon dioxide or methane, which are primary contributors to global warming and climate change. Additionally, fusion power does not produce long-lived radioactive waste, as nuclear fission reactors do, minimizing the risk of nuclear proliferation and long-term environmental contamination.

Furthermore, fusion power has the potential to revolutionize global energy systems by providing a reliable, baseload source of electricity that is not subject to fluctuations in fuel prices or geopolitical tensions. Fusion reactors can operate continuously for long periods, generating steady, predictable power with high availability and low operating costs. This reliability and stability make fusion power an attractive option for meeting the growing energy demands of an increasingly electrified and interconnected world.

Challenges and Future Prospects

Despite its immense potential, fusion power faces numerous technical, economic, and regulatory challenges that must be overcome before it can become a commercially viable energy source. One of the primary challenges is achieving and sustaining the extreme conditions required for nuclear fusion to occur, including temperatures of over 100 million degrees Celsius and pressures millions of times greater than atmospheric pressure.

Currently, the most promising approach to achieving controlled nuclear fusion is through magnetic confinement fusion (MCF), which uses powerful magnetic fields to confine and heat a plasma of hydrogen isotopes to the temperatures and pressures required for fusion reactions to occur. The leading MCF technology is the tokamak, a doughnut-shaped device that confines the plasma within a toroidal magnetic field, such as the ITER (International Thermonuclear Experimental Reactor) project, a multinational fusion research initiative currently under construction in France.

Another approach to achieving controlled nuclear fusion is inertial confinement fusion (ICF), which uses high-power lasers or particle beams to rapidly compress and heat a small pellet of hydrogen isotopes to the conditions required for fusion. The most prominent ICF facility is the National Ignition Facility (NIF) at Lawrence Livermore National Laboratory in the United States, which aims to achieve self-sustaining fusion reactions through laser-driven implosion experiments.

In addition to technical challenges, fusion power also faces significant economic and regulatory hurdles that must be addressed to realize its full potential. Fusion research and development require substantial investments in infrastructure, materials, and human capital, with costs running into the billions of dollars over decades-long timeframes. Moreover, the commercialization of fusion power will require regulatory approval, public acceptance, and market adoption, as well as competition with established energy sources, such as fossil fuels and nuclear fission.

Despite these challenges, the prospects for fusion power are brighter than ever, thanks to advances in fusion science, engineering, and technology, as well as growing global recognition of the urgent need to transition to sustainable, low-carbon energy sources. Fusion research and development efforts are progressing rapidly, with significant milestones achieved in plasma confinement, heating, and stability, as well as materials science, reactor design, and fusion diagnostics.

Moreover, the increasing availability of public and private funding, along with international collaboration and coordination, is accelerating progress towards practical fusion energy. Initiatives such as ITER, NIF, and private fusion startups, such as TAE Technologies, Commonwealth Fusion Systems, and General Fusion, are leading the way in advancing fusion research and development, bringing us closer to the realization of commercial fusion power.

Chapter 17

Blockchain Technology

Introduction to Blockchain Technology

Blockchain technology has emerged as a transformative innovation with the potential to revolutionize various industries and applications, ranging from finance and supply chain management to healthcare and digital identity. At its core, blockchain is a decentralized, distributed ledger technology that enables secure, transparent, and tamper-resistant record-keeping of transactions and data. Unlike traditional centralized databases, which rely on a single trusted authority to maintain and verify records, blockchain operates on a peer-to-peer network of computers, or nodes, where each participant maintains a copy of the ledger and collaborates to validate and record transactions in a transparent and immutable manner.

Security and Automation Applications

One of the key features of blockchain technology is its inherent security and immutability, which make it well-suited for a wide range of security and automation applications. By leveraging cryptographic techniques, consensus mechanisms, and decentralized governance models, blockchain enables trustless and transparent transactions without the need for intermediaries or central authorities. This makes blockchain ideal for applications where security, transparency, and auditability are paramount, such as financial transactions, supply chain management, and identity verification.

In finance, blockchain technology is revolutionizing the way financial transactions are conducted, recorded, and verified. By using distributed ledger technology, blockchain eliminates the need for centralized financial institutions, such as banks and clearinghouses, to facilitate transactions, reducing costs, delays, and risks associated with traditional financial systems. Blockchain-based cryptocurrencies, such as Bitcoin and Ethereum, enable peer-to-peer transactions without the need for intermediaries, allowing users to send and receive payments quickly, securely, and transparently, regardless of geographic location or traditional banking infrastructure.

Moreover, blockchain technology is enabling the automation of complex business processes through the use of smart contracts, which are self-executing contracts with the terms of the agreement directly written into code. Smart contracts automatically enforce the terms of the agreement, execute predefined actions, and trigger transactions when specified conditions are met, eliminating the need for intermediaries, reducing errors, and increasing efficiency. Smart contracts have applications across various industries, including supply chain management, insurance, real estate, and digital rights management, where automation, transparency, and trust are critical for ensuring compliance and reducing friction in business processes.

Furthermore, blockchain technology is revolutionizing supply chain management by providing a transparent and immutable record of the provenance, ownership, and movement of goods and assets throughout the supply chain. By using blockchain-based systems, companies can track the production, shipment, and delivery of products in real-time, verify the authenticity and quality of goods, and ensure compliance with regulatory requirements and industry standards. Blockchain-based supply chain solutions offer benefits such as enhanced traceability, reduced counterfeiting, improved inventory management, and increased efficiency in logistics and procurement processes.

Additionally, blockchain technology has applications in digital identity management, where it enables individuals to securely store, manage, and share their digital identities and credentials in a decentralized and privacy-preserving manner. Blockchain-based identity solutions use cryptographic techniques to create unique digital signatures, or hashes, for each identity record, which can be verified and authenticated by trusted parties without revealing sensitive personal information. Blockchain-based identity systems offer benefits such as enhanced security, privacy, and control over personal data, reducing the risk of identity theft, fraud, and unauthorized access to sensitive information.

Impacts on Finance and Digital Identity

The adoption of blockchain technology is reshaping the financial landscape by democratizing access to financial services, reducing barriers to entry, and empowering individuals to take control of their financial assets and transactions. Blockchain-based cryptocurrencies, such as Bitcoin and Ethereum, enable peer-to-peer transactions without the need for intermediaries, allowing users to send and receive payments quickly, securely, and transparently, regardless of geographic location or traditional banking infrastructure. Moreover, blockchain-based smart contracts enable the automation of complex financial transactions, such as loans, derivatives, and asset transfers, reducing costs, delays, and risks associated with traditional financial systems.

Furthermore, blockchain technology has the potential to revolutionize digital identity management by providing individuals with secure, privacy-preserving, and self-sovereign control over their digital identities and credentials. Blockchain-based identity solutions use cryptographic techniques to create unique digital signatures, or hashes, for each identity record, which can be verified and authenticated by trusted parties without revealing sensitive personal information.

Blockchain-based identity systems offer benefits such as enhanced security, privacy, and control over personal data, reducing the risk of identity theft, fraud, and unauthorized access to sensitive information.

Chapter 18

Solid-State Batteries

Introduction to Solid-State Batteries

Solid-state batteries represent a significant advancement in energy storage technology, offering numerous advantages over traditional lithium-ion batteries and other conventional energy storage solutions. Unlike conventional batteries, which use liquid or gel electrolytes, solid-state batteries employ solid electrolytes, providing increased energy density, improved safety, and enhanced stability. This article explores the advantages of solid-state batteries over traditional batteries and their potential applications in energy storage systems.

Advantages Over Traditional Batteries

Solid-state batteries offer several key advantages over traditional lithium-ion batteries, including:

1. Improved Safety: One of the most significant advantages of solid-state batteries is their enhanced safety compared to traditional batteries. Traditional lithium-ion batteries are prone to thermal runaway and fire hazards due to the flammable liquid electrolytes used in their construction. In contrast, solid-state batteries use non-flammable solid electrolytes, reducing the risk of thermal runaway and enhancing overall safety.

2. Higher Energy Density: Solid-state batteries have higher energy densities compared to traditional batteries, allowing them to store more energy in a smaller and lighter package. This increased energy density enables the development of smaller, lighter, and more energy-efficient devices and electric vehicles (EVs) with longer driving ranges.

3. Improved Cycle Life: Solid-state batteries exhibit improved cycle life and durability compared to traditional batteries. Traditional lithium-ion batteries degrade over time due to the formation of lithium dendrites, which can cause short circuits and reduce battery performance. Solid-state batteries are less prone to dendrite formation, resulting in longer cycle life and improved reliability.

4. Enhanced Stability: Solid-state batteries offer enhanced chemical and thermal stability compared to traditional batteries. Traditional lithium-ion batteries are susceptible to degradation and performance loss at high temperatures, limiting their applicability in demanding environments. Solid-state batteries can operate at higher temperatures without compromising performance, making them suitable for a wide range of applications, including automotive, aerospace, and renewable energy storage.

5. Reduced Environmental Impact: Solid-state batteries have the potential to reduce the environmental impact of energy storage systems compared to traditional batteries. Traditional lithium-ion batteries rely on rare and environmentally harmful materials, such as cobalt and nickel, for their construction. Solid-state batteries can be manufactured using more abundant and environmentally friendly materials, reducing reliance on scarce resources and minimizing environmental degradation.

Potential Applications in Energy Storage

Solid-state batteries have the potential to revolutionize energy storage systems across various applications, including:

1. Electric Vehicles (EVs): Solid-state batteries hold great promise for powering the next generation of electric vehicles (EVs). Their higher energy density, improved safety, and longer cycle life make them ideal for use in EVs, enabling longer driving ranges, faster charging times, and increased durability. Solid-state batteries could accelerate the adoption of EVs by addressing key limitations associated with traditional lithium-ion batteries, such as range anxiety and battery degradation.

2. Portable Electronics: Solid-state batteries can enhance the performance and reliability of portable electronics, such as smartphones, laptops, and wearable devices. Their higher energy density and improved safety make them well-suited for powering high-performance devices with longer battery life and reduced risk of overheating or fire hazards. Solid-state batteries could enable the development of thinner, lighter, and more energy-efficient consumer electronics with enhanced functionality and longevity.

3. Grid-Scale Energy Storage: Solid-state batteries have the potential to transform grid-scale energy storage systems by providing reliable, efficient, and cost-effective storage solutions for renewable energy sources, such as solar and wind power. Their higher energy density, improved cycle life, and enhanced stability make them suitable for storing large quantities of energy generated from renewable sources and delivering it to the grid when needed. Solid-state batteries could facilitate the transition to a more sustainable and resilient energy infrastructure by mitigating the intermittency and variability of renewable energy generation.

4. Aerospace and Aviation: Solid-state batteries could revolutionize the aerospace and aviation industries by providing lightweight, high-performance energy storage solutions for aircraft and spacecraft. Their higher energy density, improved safety, and enhanced stability make them ideal for powering electric propulsion systems, unmanned aerial vehicles (UAVs), and satellites. Solid-state batteries could enable the development of more efficient, reliable, and environmentally friendly aerospace vehicles with reduced fuel consumption and emissions.

5. Stationary Storage: Solid-state batteries can be used for stationary energy storage applications, such as backup power systems, microgrids, and energy storage installations for homes and businesses. Their higher energy density, improved cycle life, and enhanced stability make them well-suited for storing excess energy generated from renewable sources, such as solar panels and wind turbines, and providing reliable power during grid outages or peak demand periods. Solid-state batteries could help improve energy resiliency, reduce reliance on fossil fuels, and promote the transition to a more sustainable and decentralized energy infrastructure.

Conclusion

In conclusion, emerging technologies such as blockchain, fusion power, 3D printing, and artificial intelligence are poised to reshape the world in profound and transformative ways. These technologies hold the promise of addressing some of the most pressing challenges facing humanity, from climate change and energy sustainability to healthcare and digital security.

Blockchain technology, with its decentralized, transparent, and tamper-resistant ledger system, has the potential to revolutionize industries such as finance, supply chain management, and digital identity. By enabling trustless transactions and automation through smart contracts, blockchain can reduce costs, increase efficiency, and empower individuals to take control of their financial assets and personal data.

Fusion power represents a clean, safe, and virtually limitless source of energy that could help address the growing energy demands of a rapidly expanding global population while mitigating the adverse effects of climate change and environmental degradation. Although significant technical, economic, and regulatory challenges remain, advances in fusion research and development offer hope for practical fusion energy in the coming decades.

3D printing technology is revolutionizing manufacturing by enabling rapid prototyping, customization, and decentralized production of complex objects across various industries. With advancements in materials, processes, and applications, 3D printing has the potential to democratize manufacturing, reduce waste, and unlock new opportunities for innovation and creativity.

Artificial intelligence, particularly artificial general intelligence (AGI), holds the promise of creating machines with human-like intelligence and problem-solving capabilities. AGI has the potential to revolutionize fields such as healthcare, education, and transportation, but also raises ethical, social, and existential questions about the implications of creating intelligent machines that surpass human capabilities.

As these emerging technologies continue to evolve and mature, it is essential to consider their potential impacts on society, economy, and the environment. Ethical considerations, regulatory frameworks, and responsible innovation are crucial for ensuring that these technologies are developed and deployed in a manner that maximizes their benefits while minimizing risks and unintended consequences.

www.ingramcontent.com/pod-product-compliance
Lightning Source LLC
Chambersburg PA
CBHW071208240526
45470CB00018B/1599